RAIL REPLACEMENT BUSES: LONDON AND THE SOUTH EAST

MALCOLM BATTEN

AMBERLEY

First published 2023

Amberley Publishing
The Hill, Stroud
Gloucestershire, GL5 4EP

www.amberley-books.com

Copyright © Malcolm Batten, 2023

The right of Malcolm Batten to be identified
as the Author of this work has been asserted in
accordance with the Copyrights, Designs and
Patents Act 1988.

ISBN 978 1 3981 0868 4 (print)
ISBN 978 1 3981 0869 1 (ebook)

British Library Cataloguing in Publication Data.
A catalogue record for this book is available from
the British Library.

Origination by Amberley Publishing.
Printed in the UK.

Introduction

Londoners, and London-bound commuters, rely heavily on the railways, London Underground and Docklands Light Railway to get around. London's buses, trams, trolleybuses and Underground were brought under common public ownership in 1933 when London Transport was formed, holding a monopoly over an area that was to cover not only what would later become Greater London but also a country area extending well into the home counties. The main line railways were also nationalised as British Railways in 1948.

Since then, there have been various changes in ownership. In 1970 the London Transport country area and Green Line services were hived off to the recently created National Bus Company as London Country Bus Services. The central area red buses and Underground came under the auspices of the Greater London Council. But this would fall out of favour under the Conservative government of Margaret Thatcher and was abolished. From 29 June 1984 a new body, London Regional Transport, took over London Transport from the GLC. Then, from 1 April 1985, the new wholly owned subsidiary London Buses Ltd took on the operation of buses, with a separate subsidiary to run the Underground.

Later, in 1989, also under the Conservative philosophy, London Buses was split into eleven regional operating units, plus London Coaches who ran the sightseeing operation. This was in preparation for eventual privatisation in the 1990s. Nationally, deregulation and route tendering were introduced in October 1986, and the National Bus Company fleets were split up and privatised. In the 1990s the state-owned British Railways was also privatised with different train-operating companies bidding for franchises to run passenger services. The track infrastructure was placed in the hands of a separate company, Railtrack, since replaced by Network Rail. At least the London Underground remained under single ownership, although since 1987 London now also had the growing Docklands Light Railway, run separately under franchise.

Since 2000, the ownership system has changed again with the election of a London mayor, who has responsibility for public transport in his remit. The bus licensing, the Underground (from July 2003) and DLR all eventually came under direction from a new body named Transport for London (TfL). Although the mayor does not control the train-operating companies, since November 2007 some of their services have been transferred to a new London Overground network, which is part of TfL. These lines all have their service levels, fares and conditions regulated by TfL and accept the popular Oyster cards that were introduced in 2003.

New investment has taken place on the main lines, DLR and Underground network to keep up with London's population growth and as a result of the redevelopment of Docklands and the award of the Olympic Games to London in 2012. Rail travel nationally has grown substantially since the doldrum days of the 1960s and 1970s when closures were the norm rather than investment.

But, of course, there is a constant need for maintenance, and sections of lines are often closed at weekends and bank holidays for track work and other enhancements to take place. These times are to avoid disrupting commuter traffic. Closures mean rail replacement buses whenever there is not an easy alternative rail route. The logistics of railway operation usually requires a closure of a much longer section of line than that actually being worked on. On double-track routes trains require a location where they can reverse onto the other line to make the return journey. Not all stations have this facility, and this is particularly the case on the deep tunnel sections of the Underground where the tracks are in separate bores. Thus, on the Central line track replacement at, say, Holborn may mean a closure from Liverpool Street to Marble Arch, as these are the nearest places where trains can reverse. However, often closures of sections of the Underground in the Central London area do not need rail replacement buses as there are sufficient other nearby lines and bus routes to carry the traffic.

Elsewhere, the provision of rail replacement buses is a complicated logistical problem that requires much advance planning and co-ordination. Intended closures need to be notified to the travelling public well in advance. Line closures will be co-ordinated so that alternative routes are available for through passengers where possible. Where replacement buses are in use, routes must be planned. Some stations may not be able to be served directly because of their locations. There may be low bridges preventing double-deck vehicles from being used. There will need to be space at the ends of routes for vehicles to lay over while drivers take their breaks, and such factors will dictate the start and end points for replacement services.

Sometimes engineering work at a critical location can affect lines over a large area. For instance, during Crossrail construction there was major track restructuring at the busy junction station of Shenfield on the line from Liverpool Street, closing all lines. This meant no trains from Liverpool Street on local, outer suburban and main line services on many weekends over a distance of 20-plus miles. Replacement buses and coaches ran from Newbury Park station on the Central line, which has a vast car park and is located on the A12 Eastern Avenue main road. From here, replacement services ran to Ingatestone (for Chelmsford and beyond), Billericay (for stations to Southend) and Romford and Shenfield for local passengers. Another bus service replaced local trains between Romford and Stratford where passengers could transfer to the Underground for Liverpool Street and beyond.

Major investment projects, such as electrification or tunnel repairs, may require the closure of a line for a longer continuous period involving weekdays and all the peak-hour traffic that may entail. A dedicated long-term replacement will then be put in place, which may involve vehicles carrying a special livery for the duration – weeks, months or even years.

Probably the earliest example of a dedicated railway replacement service in London was in 1922 when parts of the City & South London Railway (now the Northern line) were closed for tunnel enlargement and modernisation. A fleet of sixteen B-type buses in a blue livery were initially used between Euston and Moorgate. From January 1923 the service ran from Moorgate to Clapham Common and forty-six buses were required. Vehicles ran at one-minute intervals, stopping only at Tube stations.

From the days of London Transport until 1984 the buses and Underground were both LT owned, so London buses would be used for Underground replacement. There would be spare buses available at weekends, particularly on Sundays in the days before Sunday shopping. Between 1985 and 2000 there were many companies operating tendered London Bus services and, until restrictions were imposed, in a whole variety of liveries, and many of these would provide rail replacement services. When London Buses was split into separate companies, these also provided rail replacement services, and this continued after they were privatised. To supplement these companies a variety of bus operators and vehicles were used. Often these were companies from around the Home Counties, whose buses were employed on local routes or school contracts during the week and whose drivers were willing to earn some weekend overtime. Certain companies, especially Blue Triangle, Capital Citybus and Ensignbus, became masters at co-ordinating rail replacement services and thus became the lead contractors, sub-contracting these other companies to supplement their own vehicles.

Since July 2003, under TfL, there has been common overall responsibility for the red buses and the Underground (and now also DLR and London Overground). Since 1996 the work has been put out to tender by London Buses on behalf of London Underground and, naturally, the privatised companies that operate London bus services will tender, and their vehicles are primarily used for rail replacement on these lines. In February 2003, TfL issued an edict that buses used on LUL replacements should only come from TfL route contractors. However, circumstances mean that these will still need to be supplemented by others as required.

British Railways would often use London Transport vehicles within their area, and other local companies elsewhere. Since privatisation, the train-operating companies (TOCs) will hire in vehicles from a variety of companies, including London Transport's successors. Some of these also have bus interests; Arriva, FirstGroup and Stagecoach all have both road and rail operations and so tend to use vehicles from their bus companies. For instance, South West Trains was owned by Stagecoach, who have bus subsidiaries nationally, so they would frequently use vehicles from their own fleets. They had some vehicles painted in South West Trains livery specifically for this work.

As many of the National Rail replacement journeys may involve longer distances than is the case with the Underground, often coaches rather than buses will be employed. These are also better equipped to convey passengers' luggage and may be fitted with toilets.

The quantity of vehicles involved can vary enormously from just a handful for a minor branch line job to hundreds of vehicles for a major closure of a section of main line or a long section of the Underground where there are few alternative routes, such as the Central line to Epping, especially if weekday rush hours are to be included. Sometimes there will be buses running non-stop between the end points to convey through passengers and others stopping at the intermediate stations. At the other end of the scale, a minor station on a line may be bypassed by the replacement service and intending passengers conveyed there by a minibus or taxi.

Since 2017, buses on stage services have been required to be fully accessible. Rail carriages and Underground cars are also generally accessible, although many stations do not have step-free access to platforms and/or trains, and in some cases this may not be achievable. The Docklands Light Railway has always been fully accessible. It has been the intention to make all vehicles used on rail replacement services accessible. Indeed, the deadline for this had been extended twice, and was set at 30 April 2020. However, with the coronavirus pandemic disrupting everything, this was put back until the end of 2020. Obviously, where buses off stage services are used this is not a problem, but many old school buses and most coaches would fall foul of this legislation. Therefore, in 2020 some coach operators bought low-floor buses to ensure they could continue with this lucrative rail replacement work. Meanwhile, the policies of the various train-operating companies towards provision and accessibility can be found on the National Rail website as well as their individual sites. For instance, on the National Rail website it states, 'All rail replacement services will display the destination, train company name and "RAIL REPLACEMENT" wording.'

Finally, there are the unforeseen closures – perhaps due to derailments or signalling failures or through the forces of nature (flooding, landslips, etc.). A major technical fault may occasionally mean trains have to be withdrawn for a period for modifications. Industrial action can also lead to the suspension of services. In such cases, buses may be brought in at short notice until services can be restored, and at such times vehicles may come from far and wide and may well include veterans from bus companies' heritage fleets.

This book features various planned and emergency rail replacement services around London and the South East over the last fifty years, although mainly following deregulation and privatisation. The photographs have been selected to show the wide variety of companies and vehicle types engaged on such work. All photographs are by the author.

Flashback – British Rail Replacements in the 1970s

London Transport RT2275 leads a trio of similar buses on rail replacement for the Barking–Kentish Town line at Leytonstone High Road station on 15 February 1970. Considering the trains would normally be a two- or three-car DMU, three buses seems a bit excessive for the likely number of passengers.

Wilts & Dorset Bristol FLF6B No. 686 stands at Reading station ready to work a rail replacement service to its home town of Basingstoke. 27 March 1971.

London Transport AEC Swift SMS576 at Walthamstow Central on 8 August 1971 with a replacement service on the BR Chingford line.

London Transport Red Arrow AEC Merlin MBA535 stands in the forecourt of Charing Cross Station on BR rail replacement duty on 19 April 1976. All the LT vehicles are showing the printed blind display 'RAILWAY EMERGENCY SERVICE'.

Routine Weekend British Rail/National Rail/London Overground Replacements

Eastern Counties Bristol VR buses wait at Manningtree station for passengers on a replacement service – probably to Ipswich. 9 September 1984.

London General Fleetline DMS2310 awaits departure at Hampton Court on 29 March 1991, probably conveying passengers to Surbiton, the junction station on the main line, calling at the one intermediate station of Thames Ditton.

Selkent Leyland Olympian L9 was at Eltham station 4 April 1992. The windscreen label shows that it was working to Plumstead, which it will reach following the loop line stations via Barnehurst and Erith.

A replacement service from Stratford on 6 June 1993 was contracted to Harris, Grays. Among the vehicles they provided was this ex-Southdown 'Queen Mary' Leyland PD3/4 with Northern Counties convertible open-top bodywork.

On the same day was D304 PEV, one of four Volvo B9Ms with Plaxton B38F bodies bought new in 1986.

Subcontracted by Harris was S&M Coaches (Castlepoint) KUC 941P, formerly London Transport DMS1941with Metro-Cammell bodywork.

Rail replacement over the same route was also in place on 27 June and among the vehicles brought in by Harris on this occasion was Eastbourne Corporation 25, G25 HDW. This was one of two 1990 Dennis Javelins with Duple 300 B55F bodies acquired from Bebb, Llantwit Fardre in 1991.

Bank holidays are a popular time for rail replacement as it gives three days to get the work done. On 29 August 1993 the Great Eastern main line was out between Romford and Ingatestone, probably for trackwork or signalling at Shenfield. A pair of Colchester Corporation Leyland Atlanteans with ECW bodywork wait to depart from Romford station. Note the printed blinds.

While passengers for Chelmsford and beyond were conveyed to Ingatestone, those for the Southend and Southminster lines were bussed to Wickford. Southend Corporation Daimler Fleetline 254 loads for Wickford. Note the registration – Q554 MEV. This was one of three 1972 Fleetlines that were rebuilt and rebodied by Northern Counties in 1985 and considered so modified that they were allocated new registration numbers in the Q series then used for rebuilds and vehicles of indeterminate age. Originally this was No. 376 GHJ 376L.

Back at Stratford again, this time on 27 March 1994 and Harris Bus have subcontracted MRR 804K from S&M Coaches. This is a 1972 AEC Reliance new to Barton Transport but latterly with London Country as RN3. The 3+2 seating in its Plaxton body could take sixty passengers. A Harris Bus Bristol VR with Alexander body is behind – new to Northampton Corporation.

At Newbury Park station on 29 March 1997 is a Bristol VR of Stephensons. MFA 719V began life with Potteries Motor Traction in 1980.

At Cobham station on 26 October 1997, this Tillingbourne bus is working for the now privatised South West Trains franchise, although the blinds say British Rail. L104 EPA is a 1994 Volvo B6-50 with Northern Counties Paladin B40F body.

Also from Tillingbourne and seen at Woking station in January 1999 is H683 GPF. This is a 1991 Volvo Citybus with East Lancs bodywork, one of three in the fleet at the time. Note the blinds now saying 'On hire to South West Trains'.

We are back at Eltham station in January 2001. This Duple-bodied coach of Owens Coaches, Sidcup, is working for the train operator Connex and is going to Abbey Wood. A notice in the windscreen reads 'Connex rail ticket holders only'.

At Surbiton in April 2003 and we have Countryliner from Guildford. The coach is a Plaxton-bodied Leyland Tiger new to Shamrock & Rambler. Beside it is former London Transport T406 with Thomas, West Ewell. South West Trains are the rail company affected.

At Strood, on 20 April 2003, Kings Ferry vehicles are replacing Conex trains on the Medway Valley line to Maidstone. H208 LOM is a 1990 Scania N113DR with Alexander bodywork, ex-West Midlands 3208.

This Alexander-bodied Volvo B6 of Central Parking Services (t/a Centra) was at Tolworth station with a South West Trains replacement service to Surbiton. 3 April 2005.

The South West Trains franchise was held by the Stagecoach Group, who painted some of their buses into the railway livery especially for rail replacement work. This three-axle Leyland Olympian/Alexander was an entrant at the 2006 Alton bus rally.

Two buses from the Imperial Bus Company, Rainham lay over at Dartford for replacement services to Lewisham on 10 September 2006. A321 YWJ is an ECW-bodied Leyland Olympian ex-East Midland 321, which keeps company with ex-London Transport Titan T573.

Later in the day T573 is seen after arrival back at Lewisham. Note the LT 'mind the rush hour' notices that have been retained either side of the blind box.

The L class Leyland Olympians were the last buses new to London Transport before the fleet was split into separate operating companies. Former L126 passed to Stagecoach Selkent but by 2007 it was with Excel, Stanstead. It was seen here at Gidea Park on 25 August.

NIBS (Nelson, Wickford) BIL 4710 is seen at Brentwood station on the same day.

Stanstead Transit EU06 KOX was an Alexander Dennis Dart SLF bought new in 2006. Here it was on rail replacement work at Cambridge station in September 2007.

Arriva bought London Coaches, the first of the London Transport companies to be privatised. They operated The Original London Sightseeing Tour, mainly with open-top buses, but had some closed-top vehicles for winter and inclement weather. Cascaded from the Arriva Leaside bus fleet were these Alexander-bodied Leyland Olympians. J352 BSH stands outside Kingston bus station while working for South West Trains to New Malden in March 2009.

A major rail replacement on 28–29 March 2009 saw buses replacing South West Trains between Clapham Junction and Surbiton. Laying over at Surbiton is Volvo N779 DRH of AtBus, Thorpe, a company that started up in 2006 with school and contract services.

There would be plenty of capacity aboard Tellings-Golden Miller LJ58 GCF, a Volvo B9TL with East Lancs Olympus CH61/39F body.

Also capable of shifting the crowds is Volvo B9TL OU05 AYB of Weaveaway, Greenham Common. The rail works (at Wimbledon) continued on subsequent weekends and this was taken on 19 April.

At Weybridge station on 24 June 2012 is Stagecoach ADL Dart E200 39651 with a South West Trains replacement to Surbiton. The bus is in a commemorative livery to celebrate the centenary of Aldershot & District.

Departing from Watford Junction bus station, conveniently next to the railway station is Arriva the Shires 3413, a 2013 Optare Versa. It is working a replacement for London Overground to Harrow & Wealdstone and is branded for Watford local route 10. One of the London Overground trains can be seen in the station. 30 March 2014.

Variety at Strood with a pair of former Irish Volvo Olympians of Chalkwell, Sittingbourne. Buses from Travelmasters and London General are also on hand. 5 April 2014.

At Dartford in November 2014, Ensignbus 109 is a reregistered ex-London Dennis Trident/ Alexander ALX400 dating from 1999. There are three SouthEastern routes to Dartford and this is labelled for Plumstead replacing the northernmost of the routes via Slade Green and Erith.

A Volvo Olympian from Stagecoach in their South West Trains dedicated livery stands at the Hard bus station, Portsmouth Harbour, on 9 June 2015. It will be working a replacement service to Fareham.

A major rail replacement programme has been required when closures of parts of the TfL Rail and Greater Anglia services operated line from Liverpool Street to Shenfield occurred in connection with Crossrail building works. On occasions there have been complete line closures with passengers being bused from Newbury Park Central line station to Ingatestone and Billericay for Greater Anglia services. Ensignbus imported four Chinese-built BCI three-axle, ninety-eight-seat double-deckers in 2016 specifically for such work. One of these is seen leaving Newbury Park on 24 September 2016.

Many of the vehicles used on the longer journeys to Ingatestone were coaches such as this Volvo from New Horizon Travel of Thorrington, near Colchester. More space for luggage, but not fully accessible for any disabled passengers.

From Arriva's Southend operation, this Alexander Dennis AD Enviro400 (MMC) is standing opposite Shenfield station on 16 September 2017.

Seen near to West Byfleet station while on a replacement service for South West Trains in April 2018, this Alexander Dennis AD Enviro200 (MMC) was new in 2017. Courtney, who run services mainly around Bracknell and Maidenhead, were acquired by Reading Transport in March 2019.

Ensignbus Alexander Dennis Dart E200 No. 705 was providing a replacement service for c2c at Upminster station in December 2019.

The weekend of 29 February/1 March 2020 saw another major engineering works closure for Greater Anglia and TfL at Shenfield with no services from Liverpool Street to Ingatestone or Billericay. Replacement services again ran from Newbury Park. Trustybus (Galleon Travel 2009 Ltd) Scania N230UD OmniCity YP59 OEO departs from this station with its distinctive and award-winning bus shelter canopy. This is one of ten such buses in the fleet, acquired from London United and lettered as Central Connect for their Harlow–Epping–North Weald–Ongar service, which connects with the Central line at Epping station.

On the same day, this Volvo B8R bus of Felixstowe Travel carries MCV 'EvoRa' bodywork. The '54632' number in the blind box is the Greater Anglia duty number. The Abellio bus behind is on a TfL Rail replacement service.

Providing a local TfL Rail replacement service to Chadwell Heath and Romford is New Routemaster LT705 operated by Abellio. These buses are now frequently used on rail replacements, bringing them to areas of London that they do not penetrate in normal service.

Due to a signalling upgrade at Hither Green, on Southeastern there were no trains between Sidcup and Lewisham from 25 July to 2 August 2020. Trains were diverted by an alternative route, but a bus replacement served the intermediate stations. On 1–2 August the lines between Lewisham and Orpington were also out with bus replacement. On 1 August this AD Enviro200 (MMC) of Southdown PSV, Copthorne was at Lewisham bound for Orpington.

Also at Lewisham on 1 August this former Brighton & Hove Scania N94UD with East Lancs body had been transferred within the Go-Ahead Group to London General's contract fleet but not yet repainted and is also destined for Orpington. Note that all these modern vehicles except the London ones have digital blind displays, allowing a suitable message to be shown as specified on the National Rail website.

The latter part of October and into November saw another round of engineering work affecting TfL Rail and Greater Anglia services, so again there were major bus replacements centred on Newbury Park. On Sunday 1 November (the last weekend before London moved into Tier 3 covid restrictions) we see Fords of Althorne YN06 BUS, another Scania. This was providing a service to Billericay for Southend line passengers.

On the same day, Panther Travel of Harwich had at least three ADL Darts in use including the appropriately registered DC62 PAN. The main line was out right through to Colchester on this occasion so that was where this was heading, probably serving the intermediate stations while coaches carried passengers for Colchester and beyond non-stop. These replacements services also ran on Sundays 15 and 22 November.

Routine Weekend Underground Replacements

There are no takers upstairs on Metroline's open-top Routemaster RM644, seen on Underground replacement in Chiswick. Perhaps it wasn't very warm despite being in June 1994.

On 6 November 1994 two MCW Metrobuses from the Metroline Travel Commercial Services division of Metroline lay over at Hatton Cross station on the Piccadilly line. The nearest vehicle is M1429, reregistered WLT 826, a plate formerly carried by Routemaster RM826. The 'CS' garage code refers to Commercial Services.

Capital Citybus were regular providers of vehicles for Underground replacement services. A particular feature was the provision of colour-coded blinds for each line. Here we see red blinds for the Central line (red on the Underground map). E964 PME is a 1987 Leyland Olympian with Optare bodywork, seen at Mile End on 26 February 1995.

Another Metrobus from the Metroline Commercial Services fleet, M460, was at Euston station on 5 March 1995.

At privatisation, London Northern was bought by MTL Holdings. Metrobus M1234 is seen leaving Euston station on 12 March 1995.

This Stagecoach East London Leyland Titan, T282, was one of four (T3/233/82/8) repainted in Stagecoach's national livery style in 1995. On 20 January 1996 it was at Liverpool Street with a Central line replacement service to Leytonstone. Again, red blinds have been fitted.

Stagecoach East London restored RMC1461 to original appearance and Green Line livery in 1994. This normally worked on route 15 but was seen at Mile End on Central line replacement on 4 February 1996. After withdrawal when route 15 was converted from Routemasters in 2003, RMC1461 was donated to the London Bus Museum at Cobham.

Metroline's M1185 (with registration from RM893) departs from Golders Green for Edgware. Black blinds are appropriate for the Northern line. 10 March 1996.

RMC1513 became part of the Metroline Commercial Services fleet. Here it is at Swiss Cottage, also on 10 March 1996.

London Transport's first Metrobus M1 passed to Metroline. In April 1997 this was seen at Mile End on a Central line replacement to Woodford. It had received a repaint into original style with white around the upper-deck windows.

Same place, same weekend. Capital Citybus had adopted this red and yellow livery following London Transport Buses new ruling that buses in the central area must be 80 per cent red. No. 274 was a Dennis Dominator with Northern Counties bodywork.

Blue Triangle were another company regularly providing buses for rail replacement work. Here Titan T377, reregistered NHM 465X, is on a Metropolitan line replacement service at Baker Street station, 15 June 1997. From 1999 Blue Triangle would also be running their first London-tendered bus service.

Another of the Capital Citybus Dominators, but still in the older livery, stands at the Epping station terminus of the Central line. This displays the practice of running some replacement buses as a fast service omitting some of the intermediate stops. 29 June 1997.

This former Yorkshire Rider MCW Metrobus 2 of Motts Travel, Stoke Mandeville was photographed near Wembley Park station on 2 November 1997. The sticker in the windscreen reads 'Baker Street only' for this Metropolitan line replacement service.

Also in use was this Bristol VR from Classic Coaches of High Wycombe. XAK 911T was originally Yorkshire Traction 911.

Vehicles were brought in from far and wide for this Metropolitan line replacement between Baker Street and Wembley Park. This reregistered ex-London Leyland Titan was from Nu-Venture, Maidstone.

Engineering work on the Metropolitan line continued into 1998 and in February we see Ipswich 40, M640 EPV, a Volvo Olympian at Wembley Park station.

Goldblade, trading as London Traveller or County Traveller was a recently set up company in 1998 with contract and rail replacement work and a commercial school route in Watford. A batch of former West Midlands Metrobuses were bought and here GOG 230W emerges from Baker Street to cross Marylebone Road on 1 March.

Nostalgiabus, Mitcham operated a number of vintage and modern buses on schools, contract and heritage services. Routemaster RM1571 is at Wimbledon on 1 March 1998 with a District line replacement to Putney Bridge.

A week later, another of the Nostalgiabus vehicles passes Russell Square. B102 SED was an ex-Warrington Leyland Olympian with East Lancs DPH47/31F seating. Pity about the missing light!

This was a Northern line replacement to/from Euston, and later in the day a pair of Capital Citybus Dominators round Trafalgar Square. They will have come up from Waterloo, over Waterloo Bridge and then down the Strand.

The Dominators are followed shortly afterwards by this Stephensons, Rochford Bristol VR, which was new to Alder Valley.

On 13 September 1998 the Northern line was out between Golders Green and Edgware. Luton & District had evolved into LDT 'The Shires' and had become part of the Cowie Group, who would later rename themselves as Arriva in 1998. This Leyland Olympian is in the Luton & District colours with Amersham garage 'Chiltern Rover' branding. It is picking up at Golders Green for Hendon Central and Edgware stations only.

Also at Golders Green was Mullanys Starline of Watford with ex-LT Titan T896.

Pulling out of Golders Green station is an ex-Stagecoach VR of Classic Coaches, High Wycombe still bearing Stagecoach stripes. This started life with Alder Valley.

Leaside Buses had RMC1453, which is seen on Piccadilly line rail replacement duties at Arnos Grove station on 18 October 1998.

A 'one-off' in the Leaside fleet was this former East Kent AEC Regent V with Park Royal body numbered RV1, acquired in 1991. This was also in use on the same day. This bus has since passed into preservation.

Leaside M573, one of a number painted in this Leaside Travel livery, introduced in 1997. Again, this was taken at Arnos Grove station. Arriva closed the Leaside Travel commercial services operation in 2006.

Another Metrobus, but this one is from Goldblade (London Traveller). It started out with Greater Manchester PTE as No. 5076 in 1981.

We stay at Arnos Grove to view Colchester Borough Transport 48, a Leyland Olympian with Leyland-built bodywork to an ECW design. Colchester Borough Transport had been acquired by Arriva, who also owned Leaside.

Metroline's Commercial Services unit had been renamed Metroline Travel Contract Services in 1996 and M1185 displays the livery style adopted. It is at Richmond in January 1999 on District line replacement, hence the white on green blind. The replacement service from Richmond to Turnham Green ran for six weekends in 1998 from 24 October, then another five weekends from January 1999. Metroline were the main contractor for the service, which required twenty-four buses on Saturdays and twenty-two on Sundays.

A month later and another District line replacement sees this bus from MK Metro of Milton Keynes in use at Wimbledon. NJA 568W is a Leyland B45TL11/1R pre-production Olympian with Northern Counties bodywork, former Greater Manchester 1451.

March 1999 and more work on the Wimbledon line sees this bus from Thomas, West Ewell, in use. VJY 139V is a Leyland Atlantean with East Lancs body. It came from Plymouth Corporation.

Chambers of Bures, Suffolk, were a long-established company best known for their long trunk route from Colchester to Bury St Edmunds via Sudbury and Lavenham. Double-deckers were bought new for this service and G864 XDX is a 1989-built Alexander-bodied Leyland Olympian. On a sunny 3 October 1999 it was visiting London to help out on Central line replacement work and was noted at Mile End.

The next vehicle to turn up on the Central line service was quite a contrast. Blue Triangle had put out one of their heritage fleet in the form of RT3871 dating from 1950.

Blue Triangle often put out buses from their extensive heritage fleet and RCL2239 was also on the Central line replacement job at Mile End station on 3 October 1999. The RCLs were no strangers here, having been the mainstay of Green Line route 721 from Aldgate to Brentwood from 1965 to 1971.

We saw Colchester Borough Transport Leyland Olympian No. 48 at Arnos Grove (see p. 44)
Here are two others with former No. 49 leading, both now repainted in Arriva standard livery
following their takeover of the municipal fleet.

The following weekend, the Central line was again out and the weather was again sunny.
Another visit to Mile End and the highlight was this former BEA Routemaster NMY 632E, now
with Croftpeak.

Putney Bridge station on 3 June 2000 and London General have put out Red Arrow GLS476, a Leyland National Greenway rebuilt by East Lancs in 1993–94 on District line replacement. Note the RML behind, in normal service on route 22.

Work on replacing crossovers on the Victoria line saw a bus replacement between Victoria and Brixton daily from 5–25 August 2000. Another of London General's Leyland National Greenways, GLS486 carries a different livery style at Victoria station on 9 August 2000.

Also at Victoria a week later is London General M1432. This carries a pre-war livery style and the registration originally from RM432.

On the same day is Southlands Travel A955 SYE formerly T955. Southlands Travel was the coach division of Metrobus, based at Swanley garage.

Another vehicle on the Victoria line replacement is Travel London 410, a 1998-built Optare Excel with only twenty-six seats – not ideal for this busy section of the Underground. It carries route lettering for normal service 211.

Also on the Victoria line replacement was Limebourne with this Caetano-bodied Dart SLF.

21 August 2000 was a sunny summer day so London Central have produced open-top M420, awaiting custom at Victoria. The replacement service was co-ordinated by London General and London Central. The service ran every two or three minutes and required some fifty vehicles. The service taking place during the school holidays helped in terms of the availability of buses and drivers.

Epsom Buses, trading as Quality Line had LT contracts and local routes of their own in their home town. Here Dennis Dart K113 NGK leaves Heathrow Airport bus station while replacing Piccadilly line services to the airport. 27 May 2001.

A shorter, newer and low-floor Dart SLF is also on the rail replacement, which according to the label in the windscreen will be going through to Hammersmith.

Coaches are not normally specified for Underground replacements except for the Piccadilly line to and from Heathrow. Passengers to/from the airport will often be carrying luggage, so the luggage compartments will come in useful, as will their higher speed on the M4 motorway. These two seen at Hatton Cross station on the same day are both Dennis Javelins with Plaxton bodywork from Southlands Travel.

Baker Street station on 5 August 2001 and First Centrewest have supplied VN94, a Northern Counties-bodied Volvo Olympian. This carries branding for route 83 – Ealing Hospital to Golders Green station. There was a series of weekend replacements in August–September between Baker Street and Moorgate.

Among the colonnades of Canary Wharf in 2002 is FirstBus 605, a Dennis Dart acquired with the takeover of London Buslines and retaining their livery style.

At Stratford station in September 2002 stands Blue Triangle DN186, a Dennis Dart SLF with bodywork by Caetano. This is in their version of the '80 per cent red' requirement for London-tendered services.

MCW Metrobus M1266 carries the handsome livery adopted by London United. This was photographed near Boston Manor station while working a Piccadilly line replacement from Northfields to Heathrow on 15 March 2003. The replacement also ran the previous weekend.

This East Lancs-bodied Scania of Autocar, Five Oak Green, Tonbridge, Kent, was seen on the same day at the Hounslow East station stop.

Passing through Hounslow is former T995 now with Sullivan Buses. This company, based at South Mymms, near Potters Bar, remains a TfL-tendered bus operator, as well as having Hertfordshire contracts and a service linking Staines with Thorpe Park. They also have a small heritage fleet of ex-London vehicles. Most vehicles carry London compliant livery and they have remained regular providers of vehicles for rail replacement work.

Once again coaches were also in use in this Piccadilly line replacement and passengers alight from an Epsom Coaches vehicle at Hatton Cross. R714 KGK has Berkhof bodywork.

Passing through Dagenham on 27 April 2003, this Ensignbus MCW Metrobus 2 started out with Maidstone & District. As it is on a District line replacement from Barking to Upminster the blinds should ideally be green rather than blue.

A major replacement involving over 100 vehicles a day occurred on the weekends of 26–27 July, 2–3 and 9–10 August 2003 between Baker Street and Wembley Park (Metropolitan line) and between Finchley Road and Wembley Park (Jubilee line). The replacement services were controlled by First London. Seen at Baker Street, this ex-West Midlands Metrobus of Kelly Coaches, Hatfield, is liveried for a nightclub in Watford. As the blind box is painted over, the only indication that this is on an Underground replacement service at Baker Street is the tatty piece of paper in the windscreen.

Same weekend and the same lack of information on this vehicle from Amberlee, Southfleet. MIL 4690 is an ex-Tillingbourne Bedford YMT with Plaxton Derwent DP53F bodywork dating from 1987.

The weekend of 1–2 November 2003 saw the Central line out from Liverpool Street to Woodford. Former LT M612 of Amberlee arrives at Leytonstone on 1 November. Note that the centre door has been removed.

West Kent Buses supplied former LT Titan T671. Again, this is at Leytonstone on 1 November.

Pulling out of Leytonstone station forecourt are two vehicles from Arriva. L353 is an Alexander-bodied Olympian in the Leaside Travel fleet, while the Metrobus behind caries the 'Londonised' version of Arriva corporate livery with red replacing blue.

Working for Thorpes, B870 XYR has an interesting history. A Volvo B10M it was built as a coach for Grey-Green in 1985. In 1992 the company had nine of these coaches rebuilt with East Lancs double-deck bodies for their increasing London-tendered bus work. They passed to the Cowie Group with the company and in turn to Arriva. Note the short rear overhang. Thorpes have merely added their fleet name to the existing Arriva London livery.

LR Travel of London Colney with a nicely presented T447. It is amazing how the addition of a little lining can brighten up the overall red of London buses.

Moving on to 2010 and here is Go-Ahead London General MEC45, a 2009 Mercedes-Benz Citaro at Victoria station with a Victoria line replacement to Brixton. It is possible to travel by Southern train from Victoria to Brixton, but this would not serve the intermediate stations on the Victoria line, hence the need for a replacement service.

Standing outside the distinctive architecture of the Circle and Hammersmith & City line station at Paddington is an Arriva Shires Volvo Olympian/ Northern Counties in a promotional livery as Luton bid for city status (unsuccessfully). Behind it can be glimpsed one of London's short-lived and unpopular 'bendy bus' Citaros. May 2011.

The Green Bus Company are based in Birmingham, so it is unlikely that they had supplied this. It is more likely to have been dealer stock from Ensignbus. This was seen on 14 June 2014 departing from Canada Water station/bus station on a Jubilee line replacement.

This is Redbridge Transport school bus PN02 XCA, an East Lancs-bodied Volvo B7TL new to Go-Ahead London General as EVL12. It was in use on District line rail replacement work at Barking station on 12 October 2015. With the digital blinds fitted to this and the two previous buses it is easy to display the words 'Rail Replacement'.

Full current practice, June 2020. A weekend replacement for the District line between Tower Hill and West Ham sees buses running between Tower Hill and Barking via Canning Town (change to the DLR for West Ham). Metroline Volvo B9TL/Wright VW1264 stops at Mile End. It is fully accessible as are all TfL route buses. A suitable blind display. There is a route number DL6 for the service and this and the stopping points are shown on a small board propped in the windscreen. The coronavirus restrictions are in place so passengers will be requested to maintain social distancing on buses and trains and only travel if essential.

Although TfL tendering operators are the usual choice for Underground replacements, sometimes there is so much work going on that other vehicles will still be brought in to supplement these. One such occasion was the weekend of 10–11 October 2020 when the District line was out from Earl's Court to Upminster with replacement services from Tower Hill eastwards. There were also several closures on the London Overground. This Alexander Dennis E400MMC was from NPC (New Punjab Coaches) of Southall is seen entering Canning Town bus station on the Sunday. On the same day similar buses were noted from Westbus (part of the Metroline Group) and Westway on this service.

Routine Weekend Docklands Light Railway Replacements

The first section of the Docklands Light Railway from Stratford to Island Gardens on the Isle of Dogs had opened in 1987. Whenever it was closed for maintenance or enhancement, bus replacements were provided. East London Leyland Titan T570 finds such employ, suitably blinded, at Stratford on 4 June 1989.

London Northern M1396 from their private hire and contracts fleet at South Quay 14 April 1993.

Capital Citybus 107, a 1989 MCW Metrobus 2 near Canary Wharf in March 1992. It is heading for Island Gardens, where passengers for Greenwich can walk through the foot tunnel under the Thames.

Now part of First Capital following the takeover by FirstGroup, a pair of ex-London Transport Metrobuses pause at Crossharbour in August 1999.

Town & Country Buses, Grays, started out in 1999, taking over Ensign's local routes there. This Leyland Lynx approaching Canary Wharf station on 27 July 2002 was new to Merthyr Tydfil Transport. The paper label says all stations to Canary Wharf and the blind says 'Underground service', so this could be replacing either the Jubilee line or the DLR.

By contrast, on the same day this somewhat anonymous bus, owned by Nelson, Wickford, has the same paper label but the National Rail symbol on the blinds. As the National Rail companies have no stations on the Isle of Dogs, the situation is no clearer!

Imperial, Rainham had routes in the Harlow and Loughton area, but here this Metrobus 2 lays over in Beckton bus station while on DLR replacement. A625 BCN started out with Northern General as No. 3625. 14 June 2003.

Although Ensignbus had not been involved in London-tendered services since selling this part of their operations to Capital Citybus in December 1990, they had built up a network of routes around their base territory of Thurrock following the demise of Harris Bus. In 2008 they purchased ten new double-deckers – Volvo B9TLs with Optare Olympus bodies for these routes. They could also frequently be seen in London at weekends on rail replacement work. Here 118 is on rail replacement for the DLR and is seen in Beckton by Cyprus station, which serves the University of East London Docklands campus.

May 2009 and Ensignbus Volvo Olympian/Alexander 156 sets off from Canning Town bus station bound for London City Airport. The DLR had opened a new line from Canning Town to King George via London City Airport in December 2005. This was extended under the river to Woolwich Arsenal in January 2009.

Pulling out of Canning Town bus station on the same day, this Olympian is with TWH (Travel with Hunny). G551 VBB started life with Kentish Bus and has Northern Counties bodywork.

On the same day, I am not sure who the owners were of Olympian N122 UHP, but this was new to London United for Airbus services from London to Heathrow. This was photographed at Prince Regent station on the Beckton branch of the DLR. Alexander Royale bodywork was carried and air conditioning fitted.

The London Bus Company was the name given to the remaining part of Blue Triangle after the London contracts, vehicles thereon, garage and trading name were sold to the Go-Ahead Group in 2007. This Plaxton-bodied Dennis Trident loads at Crossharbour for Island Gardens. The DLR had been extended under the river to Lewisham from November 1999, but passengers for Greenwich and beyond to Lewisham will need to walk through the foot tunnel under the Thames from here to connect with other buses or trains. April 2009.

A rare vehicle in the fleet of TWH (Hunny). CN04 XCK is a Turkish-built BMC Falcon. Seen on the Isle of Dogs with a 'Lewisham' sticker in the windscreen this will be able to proceed to there via the Blackwall Tunnel, accessible these days only to single-deckers. September 2009.

The 'new normal'. Following relaxation of lockdown rules during the Covid-19 pandemic, London bus services had got back to near their previous service levels by mid-June 2020, but with restrictions on capacity to maintain social distancing. People were still being asked to avoid public transport unless making essential journeys and face coverings were mandatory. This New Routemaster LT776 displays an array of advisory notices while approaching Beckton with a DLR replacement service from Canary Wharf to Beckton on 21 June.

BR/ National Rail/London Overground Planned Long-term Replacements

Kentish Bus won a major rail replacement contract in 1994 when the North London Railways line between Stratford and North Woolwich was closed because of construction of the Jubilee line extension that paralleled it from Stratford to Canning Town. Two bus services were provided in its place. A double-deck service ran via Plaistow, avoiding West Ham. A single-deck service ran via West Ham, where there is a low bridge. Vehicles were painted in an attractive dedicated livery. The double-deckers were Leyland Atlanteans, such as KPJ 272W at Stratford on 23 June 1994.

The single-deckers used for the service via West Ham were Leyland Lynxes recently displaced from route 108 by new Volvo B6s. G40 VME was at North Woolwich on 31 May with the entrance to the foot tunnel under the river behind it. The service lasted until the line reopened on 29 October 1995.

Another rail replacement job in 1995–96 was for North London Railways and had routes numbered NL1–2. This used Optare StarRiders from Metroline. SR67 lays over at Willesden Junction on 29 March 1996. SRs 81,84 and 90 were also liveried for this contract.

From 17 January 2004 the tunnel between Higham and Strood on the North Kent route to the Medway towns was closed for relining and track replacement because of rock falls within. A daily rail replacement was operated between Gravesend and Strood by four companies coordinated by Ensignbus. This Ensignbus Metrobus 2 F821 YLV ex-Arriva Merseyside is seen by the riverside in Gravesend on 18 January.

Imperial, Rainham (Essex) THX 103S is former London Transport M3, one of the original batch of MCW Metrobuses dating from 1978 on the same day.

For the rail replacement single-deckers were used in a common livery of green and cream. From Ensignbus we see L115 HHV, a Northern Counties-bodied Dart new to London Northern as DNL115. The X80 number on the blinds is for the route across the Dartford bridge/tunnel from Lakeside to Bluewater and Gravesend that Ensignbus started commercially at this time. This has continued ever since, although now only as far as Bluewater. Another route X90 was initially operated from Lakeside to Dartford via Bluewater but was later discontinued.

ASD Buses provided Alexander-bodied Volvo B6s M429/32 RDC, the first of which is seen at Gravesend in 2004.

Redroute Buses had L109/116 HHV, sister vehicles to the Dart of Ensignbus. All of the buses were supplied by Ensignbus in their dealer capacity. One of these is seen later in 2005, working a local bus route.

The fourth operator was Kings Ferry and here is another of those Darts, this time at Strood station, April 2004. The rail replacement service lasted a year, train services resuming from 17 January 2005.

A major rail replacement job started in 2016 when the Barking–Gospel Oak line, now part of London Overground was closed for six months for electrification. Two bus routes were provided: the J from Gospel Oak to Seven Sisters and the T from Walthamstow Central to Barking. The latter ran every day, every 10–12 minutes on weekdays (later reduced to every 15 minutes) and 20 minutes at weekends (trains are every 15 minutes daily). Because the line runs diagonally, mainly on arches, and doesn't follow the pattern of main roads, a journey time of over one hour was required for the T (about 15 minutes by train). Arriva had the contract and here VLA161 is seen opposite Woodgrange Park station. Ensignbus also provided vehicles for route T.

A further closure period of five weeks duration for electrification work on the Barking–Gospel Oak line meant a return of the replacement bus services. This time one of the red and silver Ensignbus vehicles is seen crossing the line at Woodgrange Park station on 22 September.

The scale of rail replacement work these days can be gauged by this sight of four vehicles from three different companies laying over at Barking while on the Barking–Walthamstow Central route T. 5 October 2017.

Underground Planned Long-term Replacements

From 1 June 1993 a replacement service was operated non-stop in peak hours only between Waterloo and the Bank of England while the Waterloo & City line was closed for engineering work. Numbered 800, fourteen London Central Titans were employed. The service was sponsored by the City of London Corporation and eleven buses carried appropriate branding. T317 was near the Bank of England on 4 June.

The remaining three buses (T894, 1008/53) on the Waterloo & City line replacement service were painted in the City of London white livery. T1053 was also seen on 4 June. The service was due to run until 9 July 1993. The number was revived for a few days in April 1997 during another closure, but this time the buses were in standard livery.

A major rail replacement contract started in 1995 while work was undertaken on the East London line, which ran from Whitechapel or Shoreditch to New Cross and New Cross Gate through Brunel's original tunnel under the Thames. Route ELX ran between Aldgate and New Cross via Tower Bridge and used double-deckers provided by Capital Citybus. Ex-Merseyside Dennis Dominator CHF 350X takes on passengers in Mansell Street, near Tower Bridge, on 25 March.

The other routes were the ELS Whitechapel to Shoreditch and the ELT that ran from Whitechapel station to Surrey Quays via the Rotherhithe tunnel. Only minibuses could be used through the tunnel and Stagecoach provided these in the shape of Optare StarRiders, SR80 is at Surrey Quays on 14 April 1995. Sixteen buses were needed for these two routes.

Sometimes non-dedicated buses would get onto the routes and this is Metrobus 118 in Rotherhithe on the ELX. 29 June 1995. Eleven buses were needed on Monday– Friday.

Laying over at Aldgate is MCW Metrobus 177 DAE 513W, ex-Badgerline but new to Bristol, and Dennis Arrow P905 HMH. 20 October 1996.

The East London line replacement services were originally expected to last for six months but in fact continued until March 1998 for the ELT and ELX, September 1998 for the ELS. Capital Citybus buses lay over at Aldgate bus station between journeys on the ELX on 27 April 1997. Five new Dennis Arrows 402–6, P902–6 HMH were delivered in orange livery for use on this service.

A replacement service for part of the Bakerloo line began in November 1996 and was expected to last until July 1997. Two daily routes ran: Oxford Circus to Elephant & Castle (not serving Waterloo) and Oxford Circus to Waterloo. The work was shared by London Central and Cowie Group subsidiary Grey-Green. In February 1997 London Central Leyland Titan T1020 passes Trafalgar Square en route to Oxford Circus with dedicated blinds and posters.

A week later and Cowie Group (Grey-Green) 116 carries similar posters. This is a Volvo B10M-50 with Alexander bodywork. These were supplied new to Grey-Green in 1988 when they won the tender for route 24, but this is now repainted red in line with the livery restrictions on routes serving the central London area. Grey-Green were acquired by the Cowie Group in 1991.

The Northern line's Bank branch was due to be closed from 3 July to 5 September 1999 between Moorgate and Kennington. London Central and London General provided seventeen double-deckers as additional buses on parallel bus route 133, normally run by London General. From 14 August Stagecoach East London also provided VA136-8,140-5, Alexander-bodied Volvo Olympians from a batch bought new by the company in 1997–98. The works overran with the service ending on 10 September, but then from 24 September escalator problems caused the closure of several stations and the extra buses returned for a couple of weeks. Here VA138 is photographed outside Kings Cross station on 29 September.

The Piccadilly line section between Hatton Cross and Heathrow Terminal Four closed in January 2005 until autumn 2006. A free replacement was run on behalf of the Airport Authority by Menzies Airport Services. Scania Omnicity YN53 GGO was at Hatton Cross on 30 August 2005 with dedicated branding.

The ELS was a four-bus rail replacement route started in June 2006 for the peak hours and Sunday-mornings-only Whitechapel–Shoreditch section of the East London line, while it was rebuilt for a northwards extension to Dalston Junction. Travel London worked the route and this Optare Solo lettered for the service was pictured at Whitechapel on 10 May 2007.

In December 2007 the whole of the LUL East London line from Whitechapel to New Cross and New Cross Gate closed in preparation for its transfer to London Overground and extension northwards to Dalston. The short peak hours and Sunday mornings extension northwards to Shoreditch had already been replaced in 2006 by bus route ELS. The new ELW Whitechapel–Wapping route covered the section north of the Thames while the ELC New Cross Gate–Canada Water and ELP Canada Water–Rotherhithe worked on the south side. Initially double-deck, the ELW was converted to single-deck in 2008 and extended to replace the ELS. This short Marshall-bodied Dart was at Whitechapel on 9 August 2008. This service ended with the return of rail services in May 2010.

Between 8 August and 30 August 2015 the Victoria line was closed between Seven Sisters and Walthamstow Central for upgrading work. Three rail replacement bus routes were provided including route A between Seven Sisters and Walthamstow Central every 4–5 minutes, worked by Sullivan Buses and Arriva. Sullivan Buses ELV7 was at Walthamstow on 8 August. This was a Volvo B7TL with East Lancs bodywork.

Docklands Light Railway Planned Long-term Replacements

In 1999 the Docklands Light railway was extended from Island Gardens under the Thames to Lewisham, thus providing a much-needed alternative route to the Canary Wharf area from south-east London alongside the foot tunnel from Greenwich to Island Gardens. Construction work included the closure for realignment of Mudchute and Island Garden stations so while this took place First Capital provided bus replacements. Ex-Thamesway Dennis Dart 695 in DLR livery is at Crossharbour on 1 July.

Also in DLR livery was Optare Excel 701, again seen at Crossharbour station. This was employed so as to provide a wheelchair accessible bus – the DLR had been built as fully accessible. Vehicles in standard fleet livery were also used on this service, which ended on 25 November.

More disruption for rail passengers in 2008 was caused by platform lengthening on the DLR Lewisham branch, resulting in single line working and reduced frequencies. Peak hour supplementary bus services were provided, including links to the Jubilee line at North Greenwich. Various operators contributed to this including Travelmasters of Sheerness, as seen here at Crossharbour on 25 July with this Volvo Olympian that has been reregistered with a Northern Irish number to disguise its age.

Excel, Stanstead ex-Brighton & Hove Scania G729 RYJ departs from North Greenwich on the same day. Vehicles carried a window sticker saying 'Rail Support Service'.

Smartly turned out RM1989 came from London Heritage Travel. Many of the buses seen at North Greenwich in the morning on 25 July seemed to be running with few or no passengers, or else were going off duty.

P340 ROO had been supplied by Godward, Woodham Ferrars. This East Lancs-bodied Olympian was no stranger to east London as it had started as No. 340 with Harris, Grays, for Ilford area tendered services before passing to East Thames Buses when Harris went bust.

In full Stagecoach livery and looking as though it had only been recently repainted, this 1995 Scania L113CRL/East Lancs had now been acquired by Hunny, Rainham. Like many of the other vehicles on this frequent shuttle service it appears to be empty.

Atbus have sent S130 RLE, an Alexander-bodied Volvo Olympian previously Metroline AV30.

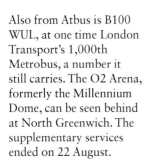

Also from Atbus is B100 WUL, at one time London Transport's 1,000th Metrobus, a number it still carries. The O2 Arena, formerly the Millennium Dome, can be seen behind at North Greenwich. The supplementary services ended on 22 August.

Emergency Replacements

A major rail replacement service started after a Central line train derailed at Chancery Lane on 25 January 2003 due to a motor becoming detached from a carriage. Bus replacements began the following day and were in force while the trains were withdrawn for modifications. Trains were restored gradually until a full service was provided from 22 April, but two bus services remained until 2 May. A wide variety of companies provided vehicles with the routes in East London being initially coordinated by Ensignbus. A total of ten different services were operated east of Stratford, with some providing links to other railway lines, such as route A, Epping to Harlow Town, and D, Debden–Loughton–Chingford. Even so, Chigwell and Grange Hill stations were not served and Theydon Bois had a minibus shuttle from Epping. From mid-February routes tended to be associated with specific operators. Drivers were drafted in from all over the country, many from Ensignbus City Sightseeing services or First Groups regional companies.

The western end of the Central line received much less replacement, only routes J, Northolt to Rayners Lane, and K, North Acton to Willesden Junction, were both worked by coaches.

Buses line up outside Leytonstone station on 19 February. At the front is ex-LT M656 now with Mediabus, Romford. The second and fourth vehicles are from Redroute Buses, Gravesend.

A most unusual model was this Neoplan N416 bus from Trustline, newly acquired and still in the colours of former owner Nelson, Wickford (NIBS). This was at Leytonstone on 19 February with a Redroute Buses Metrobus behind.

Arriving at Leytonstone on the same day is M924 TEV, a Plaxton-bodied Dart of First Essex. This carries a dedicated livery for Basildon area route 8.

First provided vehicles and drivers from a number of their provincial fleets including Midland Red West from whom came this Dennis Lance with Plaxton Verde bodywork. This was arriving at Leytonstone on route C from Epping.

From First Northampton came J115 MRP, a Volvo B10M with East Lancs body, also seen at Leytonstone on route C.

Supreme of Hadleigh provided several buses and here laying over at Buckhurst Hill on 23 March are Metrobuses originating with West Midlands (left) and Greater Manchester (middle). Route E ran Buckhurst Hill–Roding Valley–Woodford, then non-stop to Blackhorse Road for the Victoria line.

Also at Buckhurst Hill on 26 March is this Olympian of Windmill Coaches, Colchester. It is in 'as acquired' condition having come from Go-Ahead Northern.

This is a former West Midlands Leyland Lynx provided by Amberlee of Southfleet seen at Buckhurst Hill station on 23 March.

Imperial were also in on the act and M837 was at Loughton station on 26 March on route D, Debden–Loughton–Chingford.

Blue Triangle Titan T28 is at the familiar location of Newbury Park station. However, on this occasion it is the Central line that is out not National Rail, and the Titan is labelled for route H, Ilford–Gants Hill, then stations to Hainault. 22 February 2003.

On Sunday 19 October 2003 a derailment at Camden Town station on the Northern line caused damage to the tunnel wall, cabling and signalling. Replacement bus services were quickly set up and by Tuesday four routes were in operation, controlled by Ensign Bus and Blue Triangle. With over a hundred vehicles in use a day, a wide range of operators provided vehicles. Train services were restored in stages between 29 and 31 October.

A new operator to such work in London, Alec Head Coaches of Lutton, Peterborough, supplied a number of vehicles including this 1989-built former Ipswich Dennis Falcon HC with East Lancs bodywork. It was dual door with Ipswich, but the centre exit has been removed. This is departing from Golders Green.

Alec Head also provided double-deckers, including some former West Midlands Scanias. As the blind boxes had been painted over, passengers will have to rely on the labels stuck in the windscreens or information from the LUL staff.

Illustrating the vast area from which buses were sourced at short notice is this Scania from Shamrock Travel (of South Wales, not Ireland as the name might suggest).

There was disruption on the Northern line in October 2005 following concerns over emergency braking systems. The whole line was shut down on 13 October. Limited services were restored on 16–17 October with full service from 18 October. Seven emergency bus services ran, although the central London area was not covered.

Wiltax provided Metrobus M1436 working route B, Hendon Central to Finchley Road, seen here at Golders Green. Several owners of former London vehicles have tended to retain the original fleet numbers as here.

Also running this day was Sullivan Buses' former RML2272, which retains LT red livery and its former number as part of their heritage fleet. They also supplied RM1069 and RML2428.

An unexploded wartime bomb in the Thames near North Woolwich caused the temporary closure of London City Airport and the section of the DLR between Canning Town and Woolwich Arsenal on 12 February 2018 while it was dealt with. Ensignbus provided a replacement service between Canning Town and North Woolwich, where passengers for Woolwich could change to the ferry or use the foot tunnel. Chinese-built BCI No. 402 arrives at North Woolwich. Behind the wooden fence is the site of the former station goods yard – the BR line closed in 2006 when replaced by the DLR.

Miscellaneous

Because of growing unreliability and dissatisfaction with the Docklands Light Railway service, from 23 September 1991 three supplementary bus services were introduced. One ran from Mile End to Crossharbour between 07.00 and 19.00 Mondays–Fridays. The others ran from Bank–Crossharbour and Stratford–Crossharbour all day Monday–Friday. Each stopped only at bus stops close by DLR stations. To work them East London bought twenty Scania N113 buses with Alexander bodies. S28 was at South Quay on 21 November 1991. The Docklands Light Railway runs on the viaduct above the bus. These services only ran until 7 December, when they were replaced by new bus routes D8 and D11 and a frequency increase on the 277.

From June 1997 new limited stop route TL1 ran between Wimbledon and West Croydon on Mondays to Saturdays. This was to replace the Connex train service between these points, closed for conversion to the Croydon Tramlink. Ikarus-bodied DAFs were used, released by Grey-Green after they had been replaced by new low-floor Darts. The livery was red and white – the colours of the new trams that replaced them from 2000. On 24 June 1999, DIB5 awaits any potential passengers at West Croydon bus station. The route stopped at stations and at points where there would be new tram stops. The bus ran half-hourly – the train service had been every 45 minutes.

The Heathrow Express fast link from Paddington to Heathrow airport was due to open in the autumn of 1997. However, a collapse of the airport tunnel section while under construction delayed the opening. Eventually services began to a temporary station at Stockley Park in early 1998, from where a bus shuttle ran to the airport. This was operated by Speedlink Airport Services with new DAF SB220 vehicles fitted with Plaxton Prestige bodies. R984 FNM is at Heathrow Terminal 2 on 19 May 1998. Through rail services started from June.

The Jubilee line extension to Stratford opened in late 1999 and the signalling proved to be none to reliable at first. There had been pressure to get this open in time to serve the Millennium Exhibition in 2000, staged at the Millennium Dome, North Greenwich (now the O2 Arena). Vast crowds were anticipated and no public parking was provided. An emergency fleet of sixteen standby buses was assembled in case of Jubilee line failure, and this would convey passengers to Stratford or Canning Town. Blue Triangle Leyland Lynx E 678 DCU, new to Go-Ahead Northern, stands at Stratford on 3 February. Behind it is a Dennis Dart of Thorpes, the other partner in the standby operation.

A Leyland National of Thorpes lays over on the emergency bus stand at the Dome on 5 February. These standby buses were all single-deck as they would need to run through Blackwall Tunnel. The Millennium Exhibition was not the expected success, and the emergency buses were withdrawn officially by 13 October having hardly been used at a time when there was a London-wide shortage of bus drivers for regular routes.

The new Stratford International station on the HS1 high speed line from St Pancras International opened on 30 November 2009. The station is served by South Eastern with its class 395 Javelin trains. Because the station was within the building site for the London Olympics development there was no public access, so a bus shuttle was provided from Stratford station. Go-Ahead won the contract and bought eight Dennis Dart SLFs from Metroline for the service, such as R147 RLY seen here. An extension of the DLR from Stratford to Stratford International (opened in August 2011) eventually did away for the need for this.

Bibliography

Buses (Ian Allen, Key Publishing) – Monthly magazine.

National Rail for details of current accessibility policy, www.nationalrail.co.uk.

The London Bus – The London Omnibus Traction Society's monthly newsletter. This is the principal society for enthusiasts of London Transport and its successors, and anyone with an interest in the London bus scene past and present is recommended to join, www.lots.org.uk.

Various fleet lists published by The PSV Circle, LOTS, Capital Transport, etc.